Saint Kateri Tekakwitha

Saint Kateri Tekakwitha

Courageous Faith

Adapted from a book by Lillian M. Fisher
Illustrated by Barbara Kiwak

auline
BOOKS & MEDIA
Boston

Library of Congress Cataloging-in-Publication Data

Marsh, Emily.
   Saint Kateri Tekakwitha : courageous faith : adapted from a book by
Lillian M. Fisher / illustrated by Barbara Kiwak ; [adapted for children by
Emily Beata Marsh and Jaymie Stuart Wolfe].
      p. cm. -- (Encounter the saints series)
   ISBN 978-0-8198-7250-0
   1. Tekakwitha, Kateri, 1656-1680. 2. Mohawk women--New York
(State)--Biography. 3. Blessed--New York (State)--Biography I. Kiwak,
Barbara. II. Wolfe, Jaymie Stuart. III. Fisher, Lillian M. Kateri Tekakwitha.
IV. Title.
   E99.M8T4585 2012
   974.7'02092--dc23
   [B]
                                    2012024524

Book design by Mary Joseph Peterson, FSP

Cover art/illustrated by Barbara Kiwak

Based on a book by Lillian M. Fisher

Adapted for children by Emily Beata Marsh, FSP, and Jaymie Stuart
Wolfe

Prayer by Louise Hunt

Published by Pauline Books & Media, 50 Saint Pauls Avenue, Boston,
MA 02130-3491

Printed in the U.S.A.

www.pauline.org

SKT VSAUSAPEOILL9-2210166 7250-4

Pauline Books & Media is the publishing house of the Daughters of St.
Paul, an international congregation of women religious serving the
Church with the communications media.

5 6 7 8 9 10   24 23 22 21 20

*For even more titles in the
Encounter the Saints series,
visit: www.pauline.org/EncountertheSaints*

Contents

CHAPTER 1

SUNSHINE AND CLOUDS

War cries and fierce drumbeats filled the air. The Mohawk warriors had scored another victory, this time over their old enemy, the Algonquins (al-GON-kwins). Caught off guard by the surprise attack, many men were killed. The Algonquin women and children found themselves at the mercy of their enemies.

The warriors led their captives through forests and over lakes, along the trail from the wide St. Lawrence River into the valley of the Mohawks, a two hundred mile trip on foot.

As they traveled, Tsaniton-gowa (dza-nee-do-GO-wa), chief of the tribe's Turtle Clan, could not help but notice Kahontake (guh-hoo-DAHG-ay), one of the young Algonquin women. He watched with both wonder and respect as she volunteered to carry the heaviest burdens for the older women as they grew tired. This woman was different from the others, and because of that difference she was fast winning the chief's heart. Tsaniton-gowa did not know that she had learned about the one true God from Jesuit missionary priests. He did not know that Kahontake was Catholic.

When they arrived at the Mohawk village that was called Ossernenon (o-SAH-neh-non), Tsaniton-gowa married Kahontake. She soon adjusted to Mohawk customs. Being the wife of a chief, Kahontake was treated well by the other Mohawks. When God blessed their marriage with a baby girl, Tsaniton-gowa set aside his many worries, war councils, and tribal meetings.

Proudly holding the infant in his arms, he asked, "Kahontake, what name should we give our little one?"

The new mother sighed. She wanted so much to give her child a Christian name, but Kahontake did not dare to suggest this to her husband. Mohawks did not trust the European settlers, or their religion.

"Let's call her Ioragode (yo-luk-O-day), 'sunshine,'" she said.

"That's a good name," agreed Tsaniton-gowa. "She is a sunshine to all of us. When she grows older, we will give her a permanent name."

Smiling, he gently placed the sleeping child in her mother's arms and left.

Kahontake's eyes filled with tears. "Someday," she said softly, "someday the priests, the blackrobes, will pour the water of life on you, my little one. Then you, too, will belong to Rawanniio (la-wa-NEE-yo), the one true God."

"Hush! You must watch what you say," warned Anastasia, an older Algonquin woman who loved Kahontake. "If you are not careful, all of us who are Catholic will be punished."

Ioragode was her parents' delight. As a lively four-year-old, Ioragode followed her mother everywhere. She was full of curiosity and always asking questions. But more than anything, Ioragode loved to hear her mother's stories, especially those about Jesus, his mother, Mary, and the saints.

"Mamma, where do the birds come from?" asked Ioragode. She had heard the answer many times, but she loved to hear her mother repeat it again and again.

"Rawanniio made them, my little one. God made all the beautiful things of this world: the trees, the flowers, the birds, and the river; he made everything. He also made us, Ioragode.

"And because he loves us, God gave us a soul that will live forever."

"I wish I could see the soul. It must be beautiful," said Ioragode.

"Yes, and we must keep it beautiful by not committing sins."

The little girl looked down.

"Don't be sad, Ioragode. Even if we sin, Rawanniio will forgive us. He sent his Son, Jesus, to save us."

"Jesus is our brother. And beautiful Mary is his mother and ours too!" cried Ioragode with excitement.

"Yes, little one, and she loves us very much," said Kahontake. "But we must keep our love for Jesus just between the two of us, hidden in our hearts."

"Yes, Mamma, just between us," the little girl replied.

One day as she was walking with her mother, Ioragode heard strange drumbeats in the village.

"Mamma, why are they beating the drums like that?" the frightened girl asked.

Shaking her head sadly, Kahontake put her arms around her daughter.

"Ioragode, smallpox has visited our tribe."

"What is smallpox, Mamma?"

4

*"God made all the beautiful things
of this world . . ."*

"It is a sickness. When it strikes, it usually kills," answered Kahontake. "Many have died already."

"But Papa is a great chief. He will stop the smallpox," said Ioragode.

"My little one, it is not in his power. Only Rawanniio can help us."

It was not long before most of the people in the village were infected with the dreaded disease. Though he was a chief, Tsanitongowa and his family were not spared. All of them —Ioragode, her baby brother Otsiketa (o-dzee-KAY-da), and both her parents— became very ill. Because she was so sick with fever, Ioragode was not aware that her father, mother, and brother had died.

Kahontake's friend Anastasia did what she could to help. Pulling the animal skins from the doorway to let in clean air, she carried away the soiled furs and burned them. She covered the earthen floor with sweet dried grasses and swept it clean. Once fresh furs and blankets had lined Ioragode's sleeping shelf, Anastasia brought hot cornmeal stew and herb teas; she held the child while she fed her. Anastasia also applied medicine, but nothing would erase the scars from the round face of the four-year-old child.

Finally, the fever passed. In a weak voice Ioragode called for her mother. "Where is Mamma?" she whimpered. "I want to see her."

"Your mother has gone to heaven. She is with Rawanniio, the one true God, Little Sunshine. She is not dead. The *rakeni* (LA-keh-nee), the black-robed missionaries, brought her the message. Your mother was a Catholic like I am. She will never die. You will see her again one day. "

Ioragode's eyes filled with tears. "I want to be a Catholic like my mamma. She told me stories about the one true God and how Rawanniio is the only way to happiness."

Anastasia turned her head and looked back as if someone might be lurking nearby. She lowered her voice. "Remember this, Little Sunshine. You are a Mohawk and the Mohawks despise Christians. Your father's brother-in-law, Iowerano (yo-weh-LA-no), will now be chief. Tomorrow he will come into this house, bringing his wife, Karitha (ka-LEE-tha), and her sister Arosen (a-LO-zuh). His daughter Enita will now be your adopted sister. They will be your family and you must obey them. Never speak of the blackrobes or Catholics—or of Rawanniio again."

Ioragode frowned. "I will obey them and be silent. But I will keep Mamma and the one true God in my heart."

Anastasia put her arms around Ioragode. "Soon I must go back to my longhouse. I will pray for you, Little Sunshine. I will ask the blackrobes to pray for you, also."

CHAPTER 2

A NEW VILLAGE

The next day Iowerano brought his family to live in his brother-in-law's longhouse. He sat Ioragode down on the bench and spoke to her in stern words, but he also patted her hand to reassure her.

"Your aunt and I will care for you until you marry, Ioragode. When we are old, you and your husband will care for us. You must choose a good husband, one who hunts well and can provide food for the family. Karitha will bring you up to be a desirable wife. She will teach you all she knows."

Ioragode swallowed hard, dropped her gaze, and stared into the hearth. "I will do my best to be a deserving daughter, Uncle. I already know how to make mats out of corn husks."

Iowerano nodded. "You will be a good daughter, I am certain of that. Your father was a great Mohawk chief."

"And my mother was a good Algonquin. And little Otsiketa. . . ."

Ioragode fought back the tears. She wanted to be strong.

"The *okis* (O-gees), the evil spirits, have brought this upon us. Now we must leave Ossernenon and build a new village. We will call our new village Caughnawaga" (gah-naw-WAHG-ay).

Ioragode looked up quickly. "Move?" she asked.

"It is what we do when the okis come," Iowerano said, his face like stone. He got to his feet abruptly, took up his gun, and left the longhouse.

There was a hint of spring in the breeze. A whisper of fine green leaves veiled the trees. The sun seemed brighter, warmer, but Ioragode pulled her blanket tighter. From the hill she watched the flames start, the smoke billow and cloud the blue sky. She watched as the longhouse of her parents, swallowed by flames, slowly crumbled. Nothing would be the same now, and a loneliness she had never known before took hold of her. The happy life she had known at Ossernenon was lost forever.

The new village was built not far from the old settlement, where cornfields would be planted along the river's shore. Two rows of log stockades enclosed a group of longhouses. Some were a hundred feet in length and would house many families. Karitha said that the blackrobes called Mohawk towns castles. "We Mohawks are strong," she announced proudly. "The French, the English . . . no enemy would dare attack us."

Iowerano was certain the stockades would protect their castles. His longhouse resembled the old one, except it was smaller than the one Ioragode had lived in with her family. Many families had lived in the house of Tsaniton-gowa. A pair of families had shared one hearth in the dwelling's center, but there had been several other hearths. Iowerano's house, however, lodged only the chief's family.

Ioragode's space contained a sleeping shelf and a bench. Enita made her place on the opposite wall. During the day the house was gloomy as light came through only a single smoke hole in the roof. The bark houses did not have windows. But in good weather the door covering was pulled back to let in light.

Her aunts enjoyed oiling and styling Ioragode's long thick hair with ribbons and beads. They dressed her in beaded buckskin, leggings, and ornate moccasins.

"You are the daughter of a great chief," Karitha said. "You must dress accordingly." Ioragode did what she was told but had no interest in beautiful clothing. She gathered wood for the fire and kept the water jugs filled. She obeyed and helped her aunts, always with a smile, and quietly went about her tasks. No one knew of the terrible grief in her heart.

Ioragode's new father was a stranger to her. In the evenings he sat by the fire in stern silence, smoking his long-stemmed pipe, staring into the fire. His hair had been shaven on each side of his head and the remaining hair was greased and combed upward. He wore a necklace of bears' claws and another of wampum—beads of white, purple, and striped shells. Sometimes Ioragode pretended it was her own father sitting there, looking into the fire. But Iowerano's thin lips were set in a straight line, his expression like stone.

CHAPTER 3

A NEW NAME

Smallpox had left Ioragode's face scarred and her eyesight weak. But to the Mohawks it seemed that the okis had played their evil tricks on Ioragode's eyes. Spiritual matters were taken to the tribe's shaman, or medicine man. In order to chase away the evil spirits, the medicine man danced wildly, whirling and turning in a frenzy. He made frightening faces, burned sacred herbs, chanted, and shook noisy rattles.

Ioragode's eyesight, however, did not improve. The name her parents had given her meant "Little Sunshine," but now bright sunlight gave her pain. Ioragode stayed inside the longhouse most of the day. When she did go outdoors to gather wood, she shielded her eyes with her hands or pulled a blanket over her head to shade her face. She often walked with arms outstretched, feeling her way along so as not to run into trees or rocks. Doing her best to get along without complaint, Ioragode remembered what her mother had once told her: that only Rawanniio could help her.

One evening Iowerano turned to speak to Ioragode saying, "It is time we give you your permanent name."

Karitha and Arosen leaned closer. "We have thought of many names," said Arosen. "Each is fitting."

Iowerano watched his stepdaughter closely. "I can think of no name better than 'Tekakwitha'" (De-ga-GWITH-a).

"Yes," said Karitha quickly. "A perfect name. Tekakwitha means *she pushes with her hands*. Ioragode does this."

"It also means *one who works hard and puts thing in order*," Arosen chimed in.

"It is done," said Iowerano, turning again to his stepdaughter. "From this moment on, you will be known as Tekakwitha."

Tekakwitha accepted her new name just as she had accepted all the changes in her young life. Cheerfully she went about gathering wood, bringing fresh water, and cooking and serving meals to the family. Her gentle nature endeared her to everyone.

Winter came again, but the longhouse was cozy and warm. At night the chief's family gathered around the hearth. Iowerano puffed on his pipe while he stared into the fire. Karitha retold legends of the great chief Ayonwatha (a-yoo-WAH-ta) and his wonderful dreams for the *Ho-de-no-sau-nee* (ho-dee-no-SO-nee), the Iroquois. With deep attention Tekakwitha listened to the tales of her ancestors with deep attention and begged to hear more.

"An Iroquois brave had a dream," Karitha said, "a dream that gave him great power. The power gave him knowledge to know what was best for his people. It pained him to watch his people at war, tribes fighting tribes, families fighting one another. He wanted them to live in peace."

Tekakwitha's eyes grew wide with wonder. "Did he decide to help his people?"

Karitha nodded. "He dressed himself in pure white buckskin and fashioned a canoe from white birch bark. He traveled far, paddling the canoe in clear waters until at last he came to the place where the great Ayonwatha lived."

"And what was the brave's name?" Tekakwitha asked, her soft voice filled with excitement.

"His name was Peacemaker."

Tekakwitha smiled. She liked that name.

Karitha continued, "Peacemaker and Ayonwatha talked far into the night like brothers with a single purpose. They agreed that our people should lay down their arms and live in peace with one another.

"It was decided that all the tribes would be summoned to the tallest pine tree in the forest. There they would lay down their arms and bury them. The five tribes were the Onondagas, the Senecas, the Cayugas, the Oneidas, and the Mohawks—all of them Iroquois. Each tribe sent chiefs who journeyed to the tallest pine. These chiefs, or *sachems* (*say-CHEMS*) laid down their bows and arrows and tomahawks, and there was peace. The League of the Five Nations was born."

Outside, the wind howled as the smoke from the hearth fire filled the room. Tekakwitha rubbed her eyes, then frowned. It was a beautiful story. But *if it was true*, she wondered, *why did the Iroquois still make war with other tribes, and even with each other? Why did they trade skins, furs, and baskets to the Dutch at Fort Orange for whiskey and guns?*

Arosen quickly noticed Tekakwitha's expression. "What is it?" she asked. "Don't you like the story? It is true."

"I love the story," Tekakwitha said very softly.

"Then why do you frown?"

"I don't understand why our people no longer live in peace. If they accepted Ayonwatha's plan, why do we still fight our enemies?" Sadness marked Tekakwitha's face as she shook her head. "We have forgotten how to be good."

Karitha looked up sharply. "Don't speak that way. We live according to *orenda*, the Iroquois code." She shrugged. "Just sometimes we forget—*sometimes*. Always it is because of the whiskey."

"The Dutch at Fort Orange should keep their whiskey. The Great Spirit must be sad to witness such evil," Tekakwitha replied.

Karitha's eyes shone with a strange pleasure. "Ah, but you forget. There are two Great Spirits: one good and one evil. The evil one is the drinker of blood, the killer of enemies. We please and honor him when we kill our enemies."

Tekakwitha shivered, though she was near the hearth fire. *The violence, the killings, the frenzied ceremonies and drunkenness—all of these are wrong.* She recalled what Anastasia had promised, "I will ask the blackrobes to pray for you." The blackrobes taught a message of peace and love as Ayonwatha had taught. Tekakwitha caught her breath.

A wave of excitement filled her whole being. *I want to know more about the blackrobes and their prayers,* she thought. But she dared not ask questions about Catholics in Iowerano's house.

CHAPTER 4

MEETING BY CHANCE

In the forest, near the longhouse of Iowerano, a little spring bubbled up out of the ground and provided the new village with water. Violets and jack-in-the-pulpits grew nearby. Squirrels and other small animals came to drink there, and if Tekakwitha sat very still, they would come close enough so that she was able to see them even with her bad eyesight. She loved this place, and Tekakwitha enjoyed it most in the early mornings and evenings.

One early summer morning, Tekakwitha sat on a bank of moss and leaned against a giant fir tree. She was alone. Her thoughts dwelled on the prayer that the blackrobes gave to her mother. Kahontake had been baptized, and Tekakwitha longed to have the water poured on her head in the sacred rite of Baptism as well. She pondered her mother's words to her when she was small, treasuring each one, remembering the sound of her mother's voice as she spoke, softly, almost in a whisper, as they sat in the corner of the longhouse. *"Happiness comes only through communion with the one true God. He dwells within my heart, and someday, Little Sunshine, he will live in yours too."*

Suddenly, Tekakwitha heard the snapping of a twig, and she sat up quickly. As the figure came nearer, she strained to see who it was that came to the spring on heavy feet. It was Anastasia.

"Tekakwitha," the woman said, "it has been a long time since I've had a chance to speak with you. Your aunts keep you at great distance. They think I am a bad influence since I am Algonquin—and I am a Catholic."

Tekakwitha's face brightened at the sight of Anastasia. "It's so good to see you. It is true my aunts keep me away from you . . . but I must obey."

"I would not want you to disobey them, Tekakwitha, but this is a chance meeting. They won't blame you for this."

Tekakwitha's eyes shone with affection. "So many times I've wanted to go to you and ask you about the blackrobes. I want to learn their ways."

Anastasia shook her head approvingly. "Ah, Tekakwitha, I wish it could be so."

Tekakwitha moved closer. "I hear things when I work in the fields. The women talk. It saddens me to think of so much hatred. I wonder, will the Mohawks ever accept the blackrobes? Will they ever come to know Rawanniio?"

Anastasia shook her head and knelt to fill her jar with water, then set it down and settled herself on the bank of moss. "Long before you were born, the blackrobes came to bring the word of the one true God."

"My mother believed that word," Tekakwitha said eagerly.

Anastasia nodded. "Yes, but your mother was schooled by the French. She was captured when the Mohawks raided New France. She was an Algonquin slave but won your father's Mohawk heart with her gentleness and beauty."

"It must have been painful for her to pray only when no one could see her," Tekakwitha said.

"Your father knew. He commanded her to pray in private. She would have been punished if the villagers had known that she was a Christian."

"But why do the Mohawks hate the Christians so?" asked Tekakwitha.

Anastasia shrugged her broad shoulders. "Perhaps because they hate the French. When the Frenchmen came to the land of the Iroquois, they betrayed their trust and killed many chiefs. It is hard to forget, harder to forgive. The Iroquois hate the English, too, but they are friends with the Dutch because they like their guns and whiskey."

Tekakwitha bent and moved the water with her hand. It sent little ripples to the edge of the spring. "My heart cries out for the black-robed prisoners who have been tortured and killed."

"You will soon meet three of them," said Anastasia.

Tekakwitha's eyes widened with disbelief. "*I* will meet them?"

"The League has made peace with the French. It has agreed to allow a few blackrobes to come among us as missionaries. Iowerano has no choice. He will do as the council decides. Yes, the blackrobes will come."

Tekakwitha's eyes clouded with fear. "What will Iowerano do?"

"Iowerano will not defy the council. They will live in his longhouse even if it turns his stomach to have them there."

Tekakwitha brought her hands together. "Oh, Anastasia, how wonderful! When?"

"I don't know when. I only know that they are coming. You will be told when your uncle thinks you should know."

Tekakwitha nodded. "I will say nothing. I will wait."

"The blackrobes are coming."

CHAPTER 5

GUESTS IN THE LONGHOUSE

In the days that followed, Karitha and Arosen's mysterious whisperings set Tekakwitha to wondering. Enita, who was close to Tekakwitha's age, was given the task of preparing beaver pelts; while Tekakwitha swept the longhouse clean from one end to the other. When Karitha cooked a special stew in a large kettle, Tekakwitha suspected that important guests would soon arrive. Delicacies were served only on special occasions.

Iowerano peered at Tekakwitha, his expression without emotion. Pointing his pipe at her he said, "The blackrobes are coming. You are eleven years old now, old enough to serve guests. It will be your duty to tend to their needs for as long as they are in this house. I, for one, will have little to do with them, but they must be treated with hospitality and good manners."

Tekakwitha's heart pounded with a whole range of emotions. All at once she was excited, fearful, happy, and curious. Turning to leave, her eyes met the narrowed eyes of her aunt.

"Arosen and I will make ourselves scarce," Karitha said. "I have sent Enita to her cousin's longhouse. Tekakwitha will serve the blackrobes food and water. They may come here as missionaries, but none of Iowerano's family will have need of them."

The stern look in Karitha's eyes revealed her unspoken warning: Tekakwitha must not become friends with the hated missionary priests.

Iowerano's welcome speech was short, polite, and cool. He spoke for his people; he spoke for the council. It was agreed that the blackrobes should be welcomed as missionaries. Father Bruyas, Father Pierron, and Father Fremin sat together in full view of the Mohawks. Some of the crowd scowled, no one smiled. All were silent, listening intently to the chief as he grudgingly welcomed the blackrobes.

Father Bruyas answered Iowerano, thanking him for the privilege of entering the village. "The one true God is the Father of all," he said, his arms folded, his hands hidden in his sleeves. "God loves all human beings and anyone may speak to him, for he hears every whisper and sees what is in every heart."

Iowerano's expression hardened. As chief of his people, he would hold on tightly to his Mohawk religion. He wanted no part of a Christian God.

A small space had been cleared in the longhouse for the three priests, and a deer-skin hung for privacy. They were given their place on the bench, and each was assigned a sleeping shelf. Tekakwitha brought cool fresh water and served the stew with a smile. This was a feast fit for the greatest chief.

Tekakwitha, however, was bewildered by the pained expressions on the faces of the three men. She couldn't understand their hesitation, nor their reluctance to eat. They smiled and politely thanked her, but the time they took to finish the meal was exceedingly long. Knowing little of their customs, she wondered if their religion required the rakeni to eat slowly.

It was getting dark when the meal finally ended. Tekakwitha lit the fire in the hearth. Shadows fell upon the walls of the long-house, and light from the fire shone on the silver crosses the blackrobes wore. Flames brought their faces into view.

"Thank you, child," said Father Pierron in a gentle voice. "May God bless you."

As Tekakwitha cleared away the dishes, the three men knelt to pray. She couldn't understand the words, but she sensed they were important and wonderful. *If only I, too, knew how to speak to Rawanniio, the one true God*, she thought.

Bounding out the door and into the forest, she remembered what Father Bruyas had said: that God knows what is in everyone's heart. *Perhaps I don't need to speak.* "God hears every whisper. He knows what is in every heart." *Rawanniio must know how much I want to become a Christian. Perhaps he will help me.*

"Great Spirit," she whispered, "I hear your voice in the wind. Sharpen my ears to hear you better. Make my heart pure to know you and my hands ready to do your work. I want to serve you all the rest of my life as a Christian. I cannot see clearly; help me to find the way."

CHAPTER 6

A SECRET SIGN

Father Fremin left for the Castle of the Bears. Father Bruyas went to the Oneidas. Tekakwitha was happy to hear that Father Pierron would remain at Caughnawaga and share his time at Andagoron, a nearby village.

Sometimes the women spoke of the blackrobes when they worked in the fields. Tekakwitha listened, savoring every word. She watched when Father Pierron treated the sick with European medicines. She saw him pour the water upon the heads of dying infants and make the Catholic sign with his fingers.

The shaman snarled and spat words against the Christians. He shook his rattles, chanted, and danced, bared his teeth and made hideous faces. But Father Pierron just smiled and continued to serve the people. He celebrated Mass for the Huron slaves and a few Christian Algonquins. A few Mohawks came to hear him preach; some even accepted the new faith. But Iowerano remained stiffly aloof. He forbade any of his family members to speak to the rakeni, the blackrobes whom he would never forgive for bringing a foreign god to the Mohawks.

On warm days Tekakwitha would glance inside the open door of the bark chapel as she passed slowly by. She had to force her moccasins to disobey her heart and stay on the worn path that led back to the longhouse of Iowerano. Sometimes the children sang hymns. It was thrilling to hear them sing of Rawanniio. Tekakwitha wished with all her heart that she could worship with the others. She longed to share her mother's Catholic faith.

Karitha often reminded her of Iowerano's distrust of the missionaries. "When you pass the chapel you must hurry. Turn your head. Be loyal to your uncle. Never speak to the Christians."

In the evenings, Iowerano would speak aloud as he stared into the fire. "Blackrobes," he would say, "with their sick smiles and peaceful ways, poisoning the minds of our people. We must be true to our fathers and carry on our traditions. We are strong. No one in the house of Iowerano will bow to the missionaries and their lies."

Another winter came and passed. At the first thaw of the spring, Tekakwitha took her wooden buckets into the forest and fastened them to the maple trees. The sap would begin running any day, and she was old enough now to store it up to make maple syrup for the family. The syrup was especially good on corn cakes.

As much as she enjoyed watching the flow of the amber sap drip from the trees, Tekakwitha enjoyed her solitude in the quiet forest even more. Alone in the forest, she felt the presence of something holy and mysterious. She didn't know yet how to pray to him, but she sensed that the one true God was present. She was sure he could read her thoughts, look into her soul, and see how much she loved him.

Although Tekakwitha didn't fully understand what the cross represented, she knew the rakeni wore crosses, and sometimes carried a cross. Long ago it seemed, her mother made the cross sign with her fingers, touching her forehead, her chest, her left shoulder, then her right. Tekakwitha was certain the cross had a deep meaning. It was a Christian sign, and she wanted to be a Christian. She raised the fingers of her right hand to her forehead and made that sign. Joy filled her heart, and with her knife she carved the symbol of the cross on the bark of a pine tree.

Tekakwitha had kept her desire to become a Christian secret. She had respected the authority of her uncle. But now the desire to be a Christian was becoming a dangerous passion. Instead of becoming more tolerant toward the blackrobes, Iowerano's hatred was hardening. Tekakwitha often feared that he could read her thoughts. When he sat before the fire and smoked his pipe in silence, the sternness of his expression made her think he must know her every thought.

Karitha aligned herself to her husband's views. She would say, "The Huron slaves are stupid Christians. Mohawks should never allow them the choice of another religion. And they should send Anastasia away. She is an Algonquin troublemaker, and she knows no better."

Tekakwitha listened in silence. The words brought pain. She loved Anastasia as she would an aunt. But in the household of Iowerano she could not express her feelings. Instead, she would flee to the forest and kneel beneath the large pine tree, under the cross she had cut into it. Gathering her courage, Tekakwitha spoke to the one true God. She opened her heart to him and believed that he listened. "Rawanniio," she whispered, "I am here to serve you, here to love you. Make me a better Mohawk, but help me find a way to also become a Christian." She found great comfort in this act, but her happiness was marred by the fear of being discovered.

CHAPTER 7

OLD ENOUGH TO MARRY

Karitha draped strands of heavy wampum beads around Tekakwitha's neck, braceleted her arms and wrists, and adorned her hair with ribbons and beads. Even her tunic, leggings, and moccasins were heavily encrusted with beads. Her seventeenth birthday had come.

"It's time," Karitha said. "You are old enough to marry. Why do you stay to yourself so much of the time? You must attend dances and mingle with the young men."

"I am happiest when I'm alone," Tekakwitha replied, a hint of sadness in her dark eyes.

"There will be a dance in the great circle tomorrow. You must go."

Tekakwitha went to the dance, but not because she was interested in marriage. It was her nature to please; it was difficult for her to defy. She remained shyly on the sidelines, pulling her blanket over her head and shoulders. Karitha and Arosen glowered in the shadows, whispering their displeasure and frustration.

"Go to her," Arosen said. "You are her mother. She must obey you."

"Tekakwitha," Karitha said sternly, "remove your blanket to show off your ornaments. You will attract the best young men that way. You are a chief's daughter."

Tekakwitha looked down at her moccasins. "Please Aunt, I don't wish to take part in the dancing."

Karitha pursed her lips, turned to Arosen and whispered, "She should be grateful for whomever she gets. Foolish Algonquin that she is."

Tekakwitha brought her hands to her scarred, rough cheeks, and recalled what she had heard Iowerano say many times. "Tekakwitha is cheerful and industrious. The best of the young braves will be happy to make a chief's daughter his wife. Everyone loves her."

Iowerano's words brought comfort, but in her heart Tekakwitha had decided not to marry long ago.

As time went on Karitha and Arosen pressured Tekakwitha even more to take part in activities that involved potential husbands. "Please, I am not ready," she said.

"I will go to the *gan-a-shote* (gaw-NAW-sto-day) dance, but I will dance alone. I am not ready to dance with the men."

Arosen and Karitha exchanged sour looks. The tension between Tekakwitha and her aunts increased.

"You are not a true Mohawk," scolded Karitha. "You are like your Algonquin mother, weak and disloyal. Your refusal to marry brings shame to the house of Iowerano."

Tekakwitha turned away, a hurt expression clouding her face. *They don't understand*, she thought. *I am like my mother, but I am my father's daughter as well. I am a true Mohawk.*

Arosen applied Karitha's tactics, but in addition to repeated scolding, she began to demand that Tekakwitha perform difficult tasks and then complained that they were done poorly.

Tekakwitha tried harder to please her aunts, but the more she tried, the more angry and abusive they became. Slowly now her determination not to marry was growing stronger. Alone in the forest, the wind whispering through the leaves, she spoke to the one true God her mother had loved so much. "Why am I so different? Why am I not like the other girls? They wear their finest adornments and take joy in this. But I am happiest when no one takes notice of me. My aunts are angry, but no matter what happens, I cannot marry. Please help me, Rawanniio."

Once again autumn crept into the Mohawk valley, bringing the season of color and harvest. One day when Tekakwitha worked in the cornfields close to the shore, a canoe came swiftly down the river and stopped near the gardens. It carried one of the blackrobes.

Father Boniface stepped from the canoe, clutching a small box. He brought nothing else. Some of the villagers followed behind the priest; a few walked alongside him. There had always been curiosity when a stranger came to the village, and a new blackrobe was no exception.

Iowerano turned his back to the priest, again instructing his family to have nothing to do with the newcomer who had come to assist Father Pierron.

Before long the two priests built a larger chapel, a longhouse they furnished with pictures they had painted themselves, rush mats for the floor, a crucifix, and an altar on which to celebrate the Mass.

Inwardly, Tekakwitha was excited about the new chapel. She heard some of the women describe how beautiful it was, treasuring every word. But out of obedience to Iowerano she kept silent. Her longing to become a Christian was growing unbearable. As she dreamed of kneeling inside the chapel and worshiping Jesus, her heart raced with the desire to learn about the one true God.

Karitha and Arosen would not give up on the idea of finding a husband for Tekakwitha, and they were determined that one way or another she would marry. They no longer spoke to her about the matter, however, and pretended to have lost interest. Tekakwitha believed her aunts had abandoned the idea, so when Karitha and Arosen whispered and laughed together about hosting a meal for some special guests, Tekakwitha was relieved at their good humor.

The "guests" turned out to be the family of a handsome young Mohawk brave named Okwire (O-gwee-lay). As Okwire greeted Iowerano, he presented him with an expensive gift of furs. The two men exchanged smiles and nods. Tekakwitha didn't notice.

While everyone was seated for the evening meal, conversation and laughter filled the longhouse. At the height of the merriment, Karitha brought a bowl of corn-meal to Tekakwitha. Motioning at the young man, Karitha said, "Here, offer this to our guest."

Tekakwitha lifted the bowl and stretched out her arms to offer it to him. The lodge became strangely quiet. Everyone was looking at her. Tekakwitha's heart stood still as she suddenly realized what was happening.

CHAPTER 8

ALMOST TRICKED

It was as if a voice within her had spoken a strong warning; everything became clear. Tekakwitha had been tricked. These guests had come to a marriage ceremony. It was the custom among the Mohawks for the brave's family to come to the longhouse where the young woman lived. They brought gifts to her father. Then, when everyone was seated, the Mohawk girl would offer a bowl of cornmeal to the young brave. When he accepted it, the simple ceremony was over. The two were then married.

Tekakwitha's smile faded. She said nothing, but quickly set the bowl of cornmeal next to Karitha and rushed from the longhouse.

Her small feet moved swiftly down the slope to the water's edge. She settled on the sand in the shade of the cornstalks. Tears welled up in her eyes, rolled down her rough painted cheeks, and fell upon her purple wampum. It wasn't anger but sadness that filled her heart—sadness that her aunts would try to trick her into a marriage she did not want.

Footsteps padded the sand, and when Tekakwitha looked up she stared into the angry eyes of her aunt. "Come back, Tekakwitha, you foolish girl! It's not too late to repair what you have done. Do not disgrace Iowerano's house. Come back and all will still be all right."

Unwaveringly, Tekakwitha's eyes met the angry black eyes of her aunt. "I am not coming back. I am not marrying Okwire or anyone. I would rather die."

Fury burst from Karitha's face. She turned and bounded up the hill to the long-house.

Okwire and his family had left in shame. Tekakwitha was sorry for having caused her uncle embarrassment, but she couldn't help herself. She knew what she wanted, and she didn't want to marry.

Slowly she went back to the house on heavy feet. Iowerano said nothing, but he stared at her with a fierceness she understood. She had made him unhappy and angry. Karitha and Arosen became sullen and the mood continued until it was time for bed. Long after the family fell asleep, Tekakwitha lay awake on her sleeping shelf.

She felt guilty for having offended Iowerano and her aunts, but stronger for having been true to herself. She could not have done otherwise. She prayed to Rawanniio that he might make her family understand.

The next morning was no better. Nonetheless, Tekakwitha was relieved when the morning sun rose higher in the sky. It was the beginning of the corn festival, and she would meet with the other girls and take part in the corn husking. This had always been a joyful time, a time she looked forward to every year. The young girls of the village gathered every autumn to celebrate the harvest. Enita was already there in the clearing, and the husking had begun.

After a small mountain of ripe yellow maize and white flint corn had been assembled, the people carried on in a festive spirit, with songs, laughter, and joking. One of the happiest of Mohawk celebrations, this was their oldest tradition. Everyone enjoyed it.

The men sat together nearby, smoking their pipes and telling stories of glorious days past. The older women sat on the edges of the clearing and watched the happy girls. The young men watched them, too.

Because they were conscious of the braves' attention, the girls always wore their finest dresses and wampum. A few of them wore cotton dresses that had come from trading at Fort Orange, but Tekakwitha preferred her deerskin tunic.

Tekakwitha sat down next to Iowerano's daughter Enita.

"You're late," Enita said, making room for her stepsister. Already Enita had several bundles of corn beside her, twenty ears braided together in each bunch. Tekakwitha lifted a heavy ear of corn and tore a section of leaves from the cob. Her face suddenly glowed with color. The kernels were straight and plump, and . . . red!

A girl named Tonedetta who had been watching Tekakwitha since the moment she came called out teasingly, "It is a sign! It is a sign!"

"You know, Tekakwitha," Enita whispered, "the first red ear is a sign you have an admirer close by."

Tekakwitha couldn't help but smile at Tonedetta's friendly joking. It was all in good fun and was one of the most delightful moments of the harvest festival. "See," she said pointing, "even Karitha and Arosen are laughing."

Tekakwitha glanced at her aunts. It was true, they were laughing. *Perhaps they have forgiven me*, she thought hopefully. But after the laughter faded, the aunts remained sullen. Still, Tekakwitha accepted their treatment without complaint. She also continued to pray in the forest or in the quiet of her heart when she worked alongside others inside the longhouse or in the fields.

CHAPTER 9

ENITA'S NEWS

The missionaries at Caughnawaga did not pressure their hosts to accept the Catholic faith. Instead they freely offered instruction in the teachings of Jesus and the Church. The priests wanted to be certain that the intentions of the Indians who chose to be baptized were serious and sincere.

Autumn came quickly in 1670. The maples, oaks, and birch trees turned red, yellow, and brilliant orange. In the morning bark buckets mirrored thin sheets of ice on the water's surface. Winter was lurking nearby. Still there were days when warm sunshine briefly brought summer back. It was such a day when Tekakwitha, her red blanket draped about her head and shoulders, paused at the spring with her water jars. Enita had come so quietly that Tekakwitha was unaware of her presence until her stepsister spoke.

"Tekakwitha," she said softly, almost in a whisper, "I want to tell you a secret. Iowerano will hate me when he finds out."

Tekakwitha's expression revealed her deep concern. "What have you done? Is there something I can do to help you?"

"No one can help me. When Iowerano finds out he will have nothing more to do with me. I have married Onas, the Christian. Now I, too, will take the 'prayer' and become a Christian."

The news took Tekakwitha's breath away. For a few moments she didn't speak. Then she threw her arms around Enita and said, "I wish you well, Enita. You will be happy now."

"I will miss you, little sister," Enita said, her eyes glistening. "You aren't angry with me, are you?"

Tekakwitha longed to tell her stepsister of her own desire to become a Christian, but she held back. She kept the secret locked in her heart. "Iowerano will be angry," she said, "but Rawanniio will bless you."

Tekakwitha walked slowly back to the longhouse, feeling the loss of someone dear, yet also feeling joy for her stepsister.

When she entered the longhouse the fierce look in Iowerano's eyes told her that he had already learned of Enita's marriage to Onas. His words were sharp and thunderous. "None of you will ever mention the name 'Enita' in this house. Because she has betrayed us she is dead to us now."

Karitha's voice cracked with both sorrow and fury. "Ungrateful girl! After all we have done for her."

The veins on Iowerano's temples stood out in the stressful fury of hate. He picked up his musket and bounded out the door to comfort himself by hunting.

Arosen turned to Tekakwitha. "May you be a better daughter than that girl. It is the blackrobes' fault. They have brought nothing but trouble."

Knowing how Iowerano, Karitha, and Arosen felt about the rakeni, Tekakwitha worried that her family would eventually suspect that she, too, wanted to become a Christian. Iowerano had looked directly into her eyes. Could he have seen how much she longed to worship the one true God, the one he hated? She did not know. But Tekakwitha's yearning was slowly growing into something she would no longer be able to hide.

More and more she fled to the forest and knelt beneath the tall pine. She had seen the Christians on their knees and she knew this was the way to pray. "You are here, Rawanniio. I know you are with me. I want to please you. I love you; help me to love you more. Help me to become a Christian."

In the days that followed, Tekakwitha, in her shy, gentle manner, went about her daily tasks. She prepared food for the family and served it. She visited the sick and brought food to the elderly. She worked hard in the fields, planting, weeding, and tending the crops. She sewed in her spare time, creating beautiful garments decorated with porcupine quills she dyed herself. Her beadwork was intricate and fine. The whole village loved her. Iowerano was justly proud.

All the while she remained obedient and cheerful she offered silent prayers to Rawanniio. But her heart was breaking. She was not one step closer to becoming a Christian. Yet each morning when she greeted the splendor of a new day and each evening when the sun sank behind the trees, Tekakwitha asked God to help her find a way. She was sure he would.

CHAPTER 10

COURAGE TO DECIDE

Summer came once again to the Mohawk valley. Tekakwitha was now eighteen. Karitha and Arosen continued to grumble and complain, but Tekakwitha managed to avoid marriage. She had begun to believe that this was something Rawanniio was asking of her—that her desire to remain unmarried had been placed in her heart by the one true God.

Father Boniface left Caughnawaga. His health had deteriorated from the hardships of missionary work. Tekakwitha wept to see him leave, as she often took comfort from his presence in the village. On many occasions she made up her mind to speak to him, but at the last moment her courage failed her. The fear of Iowerano's anger and her loyalty to him still held her back.

Soon a new missionary, Father James de Lamberville, arrived at Caughnawaga. He was eager to serve the Mohawks, who by now had grudgingly accepted the black-robes even though they disdained the

Catholic faith. Iowerano, however, openly defied the decree of the League and refused to welcome any blackrobe who came into the village.

One day, desiring to be away from the longhouse, away from the biting words of her aunts, Tekakwitha went out to gather wood for the hearth. Though her eyesight had improved slightly, she continued to have difficulty seeing, especially in bright sunlight. She hurried on her way but failed to see the gnarled roots of an old tree that crossed her path. Before she could regain her balance, her moccasin got caught in a tangle of wood and she twisted her ankle severely. For a few minutes the pain paralyzed her. She rubbed her ankle and hobbled back to the longhouse. By the time she got inside her ankle had swelled and Karitha was forced to cut the legging.

"Stay in and rest," Karitha said. "No use to stand and work now. It will only make it worse. I have bound the sprain and if you rest it will heal. You must be well by harvest time. We will need your help then."

Tekakwitha hung her head. *If only I had been more careful and seen the roots that lay on the path*, she thought. Her aunts were kinder when she was able to work. She pleased them more when she took over their duties.

"I will sew, Aunt," she said quickly. "I will finish the eelskin bands you wanted. I'm sorry I cannot help you in the gardens. I promise to work harder once I am well."

Karitha and Arosen left for the fields, Arosen grumbling as she hurried to keep up with her sister. It had not rained in several weeks and the corn would die unless it was hand watered. Iowerano, jubilant from a streak of exceptional hunting, hurried out into the forest. Tekakwitha was alone in the dim silence of the longhouse.

On this day, Father de Lamberville was making rounds in the village to introduce himself. When he came to the house of Iowerano he paused at the open door. Tekakwitha heard his footsteps and saw his shadow in the doorway. The silver cross that hung from the priest's wide sash flashed against the dark walls, and Tekakwitha held her breath. She knew the shadow belonged to Father de Lamberville.

The pause was momentary. Slowly, almost reluctantly, the shadow began to retreat. Tekakwitha put down her sewing with trembling fingers. She wanted to call out, but there in the quiet shadows she was unable to move. *If I let him pass now when will I ever have a chance to speak to the blackrobe? Perhaps never!* She rose to her feet, smothering a cry of pain, and hobbled to the doorway.

Tekakwitha opened her mouth to speak and for a moment she seemed to have no voice. Then breathless and with forced effort she called out timidly, "It is I, Tekakwitha."

Father de Lamberville turned back and smiled. Well aware of the chief's views, he was surprised to be greeted by a member of Iowerano's household. He had not expected that a blackrobe would be admitted to this house. But now Tekakwitha was standing outside in the bright sunshine, calling to him.

Tekakwitha's breath came faster, as did her thoughts. *Do I have enough courage to tell the blackrobes that I want to become a Christian? Will the priest think I am strange?* She took a deep breath and in a clear determined voice she could hardly believe was her own, said, "Rakeni?"

"Yes, Tekakwitha. Do you wish to speak with me?"

Tekakwitha stood in the doorway, the sun forcing her to bring her hand to her brow. She squinted at the priest and supported herself by grasping the bark frame of the house with one hand.

The priest's expression changed. "Do you need help?" he asked. "I will call one of the women to help you."

Tekakwitha smiled, her courage blossoming. "It is not my ankle," she said, "only my soul. I . . . I want with all of my heart to become . . . a Catholic!"

Father de Lamberville's eyebrows came together. "But Iowerano—they tell me he even forbids anyone to mention us black-robes in his house."

"Yes, that is true. But I am old enough now to decide for myself. I want to know the one true God, Rawanniio. I want to be baptized!"

The priest frowned. "Would you defy your father to become a Christian?"

Tekakwitha nodded. "Even if my father should punish or banish me, I want to belong to Rawanniio like my mother did. Please help me."

Father de Lamberville paused in thought and studied Tekakwitha's face before he answered. "Yes, child, I will help you. As soon as you are able, you may receive instructions. I will teach you the prayer, and I will baptize you."

Tears streamed down Tekakwitha's face, but she was smiling. She could not remember having ever been happier.

She did not doubt her decision to become a Christian. She regretted only that her family would hate her when they found out.

CHAPTER 11

A TRUE MOHAWK

In the days that followed Tekakwitha prayed to Rawanniio for the strength and courage to tell Iowerano of her decision. Though she knew how angry he would be, Tekakwitha became stronger in the conviction that her decision was correct. She was determined to be prepared for anything—anything as long as she could become a child of the one true God.

Storm clouds moved in, the sky grew dark. The rain finally came, hard at first, then falling quietly upon the roof of the longhouse. Drenching the cornfields, the rain kept the women inside. Now Tekakwitha's ankle had healed, and the time to tell Iowerano had come.

Iowerano sat cross-legged on his mat, dozing off now and then, perhaps dreaming of days past. Tekakwitha sat down beside him.

"Uncle," she said gently.

Iowerano's heavy-lidded eyes fluttered, then opened.

Something came alive in Tekakwitha. An inner strength that had lain smoldering for many years suddenly burst into flames. She looked unflinchingly into her uncle's eyes.

"I have always tried to obey you, Uncle."

Startled, Iowerano stared at his step-daughter.

"That is true." Fully roused, he brought his drooping shoulders back. "What is it?" he asked, his voice rising. "I have never seen you behave this way."

Tekakwitha's gaze didn't waver. Her small body trembled, but her voice was filled with resolve. "I know how strongly you feel about Christians, but I cannot help myself. I have asked the blackrobe for Baptism. I want to become a Catholic."

Hearing these words brought anger and disappointment to Iowerano's face. His eyes bulged from their bony sockets, his large nostrils flared, and for a time he was speechless. His face, like polished leather, reflected the light of the fire as he cried out, "Ha! First Enita! And now *you*!"

Tekakwitha's eyes held his gaze with the strength and conviction of a true Mohawk. "I am sorry. That is what I must do!"

All the rage Iowerano had felt for Christians, all the hatred he had harbored so tenaciously over the years exploded into fury. He raised his hand as if to strike Tekakwitha, and she waited for the blow to fall. Instead, he threw his pipe to the floor, muttered under his breath, and rushed out into the night.

Karitha and Arosen had been listening too, though Tekakwitha had not even been aware of their presence. But now the two women unleashed their wrath, not only upon Tekakwitha, but also on all Christians. "You are worse than dead, hateful girl!" Arosen yelled. "You bring shame to the uncle who took you in when your own family died."

Karitha feigned tears. "All these years I worked to bring you up right and this is your thanks. No good will come of this. You will be punished and well you deserve it."

"Iowerano has always had a special affection for this . . . this stupid Algonquin," Arosen added. "I could never understand why."

Tekakwitha bowed her head. "I mean no harm to anyone," she said gently. "And yes, I am Algonquin, but I am a Mohawk, too.

I want to become a Christian and live in peace."

But peace was not what Tekakwitha enjoyed. Karitha and Arosen burdened Tekakwitha with even more chores and assigned her more work than she was physically capable of doing. They scolded, bullied, and abused her. The pleasant atmosphere of Iowerano's longhouse came to an end.

Several weeks passed, but Iowerano rarely spoke to his stepdaughter. Most of the time he ignored her. Tekakwitha was saddened by his ill treatment. Karitha and Arosen were anything but silent. But Tekakwitha withstood their cruelty without complaining. Every day she went to the praying house where Father de Lamberville taught her the Catholic faith. Learning about the life of Christ brought joy to her heart. However, her aunts made certain that time away from the longhouse was repaid. They forced her to awaken earlier every morning to begin her work before sunlight.

Father de Lamberville was more than satisfied with Tekakwitha's progress. "You are a rare student and a model Christian, Tekakwitha. You have lived as a Christian from your earliest childhood."

"Please, Father," Tekakwitha said, "please baptize me. I want to attend Mass and worship Rawanniio."

Father de Lamberville pondered her words and then said, "Tekakwitha, there is no reason to wait. I will baptize you on Easter Sunday."

Tekakwitha bowed her head in deep humility; tears of joy wet her cheeks. *What I've hoped for so long is finally happening! If only Iowerano and my aunts could accept me.*

Gradually, Iowerano put aside his malice toward Tekakwitha. Grudgingly he spoke to her, but only when it was necessary.

"Iowerano has not forgiven you," Karitha warned. "He will never recognize your faith. You have calmed him with your smiles and kind ways, but I see through you."

Arosen shook a finger in Tekakwitha's face, saying angrily, "You don't fool me, either. Your Christian ways will cause you more trouble. You will see."

CHAPTER 12

CHILD OF THE ONE TRUE GOD

Each day Tekakwitha's soul grew closer to Rawanniio. She continued to worship in the forest following the path that led to the tree where she had carved the cross.

"I am not worthy, Rawanniio," she said over and over, "but I want to be your child, close to you forever. If Iowerano and my aunts continue to despise the path I have taken, then I am willing to accept whatever comes. Just help me to love you more."

Karitha's and Arosen's wrath brought great pain, but for every mean and spiteful word, Tekakwitha smiled and replied with a kind answer. She looked forward to Easter Sunday with a joy deep enough to over-shadow the unhappiness at home.

The winter spent itself in one last meager snowfall, and Easter Sunday morning dawned bright and beautiful. The sun caressed the tall pines and early morning light streamed through budding oaks and maples. Tekakwitha and two other girls dressed in deerskin tunics and leggings.

With white blankets covering their heads, they solemnly stood at the baptismal font to receive the sacrament of Baptism. Tekakwitha wore no wampum, no jewelry or finery. She had given those up and chosen to offer prayers to God in their place.

The chapel was decorated with garlands of flowers and vines. The open windows let in a warm spring breeze off the river. Along with the gentle wind came the sound of birds singing. Tekakwitha stood at the font, her hands folded. The Christian name she had chosen was Catherine, in the Mohawk language, Kateri (gah-deh-LEE). Father de Lamberville poured the holy water upon her head and said,

"I baptize you, Kateri Tekakwitha, in the name of the Father, and of the Son, and of the Holy Spirit. Amen."

Tears rolled down Kateri's cheeks. Her heart seemed near to bursting. This was what she had dreamed of, the day she had longed for. Now she was a Christian! She was a child of the one true God!

Each day Kateri went to the chapel early in the morning for Mass and then again in

*"I baptize you, Kateri Tekakwitha,
in the name of the Father, and of the Son,
and of the Holy Spirit. Amen."*

the evening to pray. She did more than her share of work, but Karitha still found more and more tasks for her to do. Kateri struggled to do all that was expected. One thing she refused to do, however, was work on Sunday. This was the Lord's day.

"You are lazy, Tekakwitha," Karitha railed. "You want to get out of work and so you use your new religion as an excuse. And we will never call you 'Kateri.'"

"You are much too easy on Tekakwitha," Arosen scolded. "Those who do not work should not eat!"

Karitha smiled. "You are right, Arosen. If Tekakwitha refuses to work, she shall not eat on that day. We will hide the food. If she gets hungry enough she will change her ways."

Kateri left the longhouse and began her walk to the chapel, her head down, her blanket pulled low over her forehead. She felt the first blow with surprise. Turning, she saw a group of children from her village laughing and jeering. Then she caught the second blow on her back. The children threw stones at her and cursed. Touching her face, she felt a trickle of warm blood ooze from her cheek.

How could they do this to her? They were just children. Then she heard a boy call out, "Iowerano wants her punished. Don't stop! She is a Christian, worse than a dog!"

So, Iowerano has sent these children to bully me, she thought. *Does he think I am so weak that I would give up my faith because of a little pain?* But fear swept over her. Perhaps this was only the beginning.

When Mass ended, Kateri Tekakwitha lingered at the altar. "Rawanniio," she whispered, "you are the reason for my being. Help me to be pleasing in your sight. Everything that I do is for your glory. I love you with my whole soul, my whole heart, and my whole mind. Help me to have a perfect love for you, my one true God."

Today was Sunday and not a day of work. Kateri would, however, bring water to the longhouse. The rest of her day would be spent praying while she sewed.

CHAPTER 13

CRUELTY AND A PLAN

The breeze was balmy and the sky was bright blue above the tall pines. The grass had grown taller, so it was harder to see the wild flowers. She bent low to see them. When Kateri stood, the whole world turned dark. She felt faint and light-headed. Struggling to maintain her balance, she held on to the trunk of a small maple. She had experienced the same dizziness before. Perhaps it was from fasting the previous week or it may have been brought on by the strenuous tasks her aunts imposed.

A few times Arosen insisted that Kateri work in the fields on Sunday, and because this was a Christian holy day it broke her heart to have to obey her aunts. On days Kateri didn't work, Karitha and Arosen refused to give her food. She often ate the berries or nuts she gathered; that was all. Kateri took a deep breath and sat down to fight off the weakness.

Suddenly, as if from nowhere, a young man leaped at her, leering and screaming curses. He had a tomahawk in his raised hand, and Kateri's heart began to pound like a festival drum.

She remembered this man from a long time ago at the dances Karitha insisted she attend. But she had also seen him with Iowerano just yesterday. Now it seemed he was ready to kill her.

Kateri Tekakwitha did not speak, but instead she dropped her head and rested her chin upon her chest. Courage filled her. *If Iowerano wants me dead because I have accepted the Christian faith, then I will give my life for the one true God.* She would not be the first.

As she waited for the blow to fall she could hear the gentle sound of trickling water that fed the spring and birds singing. Kateri waited, but nothing happened. When she raised her head she found herself looking deep into the young man's eyes. The tomahawk fell from his hand with a thud, and his face fell with remorse. Sucking in his breath, he turned and ran, disappearing into the thick brush.

Kateri was shaken to know her family would go to such lengths to pull her away from her new faith. She was deeply hurt.

Still, nothing could break her love for God, not even the fear of death.

Kateri made no mention of the persecutions to Father de Lamberville, though her struggle continued day after day. She accepted this as part of her life with courage, and offered the cruelty she suffered as penance for her sins.

Kateri prayed as she always had, but her physical weakness distracted her. Her communion with God had always been an easy meditation; prayers had fallen from her lips without hesitation. Now she realized that her relationship with God was suffering because of the persecutions. She made up her mind to go to Father de Lamberville and unburden her heart. Perhaps the rakeni would have an answer.

She left her buckets at the spring and wearily walked to the chapel. Timidly she knocked at the side door where Father de Lamberville studied. The priest appeared surprised when he saw her. "Kateri, I was going to send for you."

"Then you know, Father?"

"I've learned of our visitors, if that's what you mean."

Kateri was puzzled. She knew nothing of visitors, but she poured out her heart to Father de Lamberville and told him about the cruelty she had been suffering.

"I suspected it, Kateri, but I wasn't certain."

"I would not have told you, Father, if these things had not kept my true heart hidden from Rawanniio. If even for one small moment I am apart from my Creator, then I cannot bear it. If not for that, I would have kept silent."

"Kateri," Father de Lamberville said, "God has plans for you. Chief Karonhyate (ga-LOO-ya-day), Onas, and Jacob, another Christian whom you do not know, have come to take you to the Praying Castle, the St. Francis Xavier Mission du Sault-Saint Louis. Anastasia waits for you at the Christian village. She heard of your suffering and she has planned your rescue."

"Anastasia knew?" Kateri asked, tears in her eyes.

"Someone from here brought her news of your ill treatment. Anastasia worried for your safety. She sent three good Christian men to bring you home. The trip is two hundred miles over the mountains from here. It will take two months to get there by canoe."

CHAPTER 14

ESCAPE!

Kateri trembled now, not from exhaustion or hunger, but from relief that the bullying would soon end and she would be able to practice her faith and live with other Christians in peace.

"Father, how will I escape without Iowerano finding out? He would never let me go."

Father de Lamberville's brows knit together. "Iowerano has just left for Fort Orange. His trading expeditions usually take a little time. As you know, he likes to socialize with his friends there."

"God has planned it all," said Kateri, her hands folded as if in prayer. "I will go to the longhouse and bundle my belongings."

"No," Father de Lamberville said quickly. "You must take nothing. You must not give your aunts any reason to say you have stolen anything. Better to leave everything behind. Whatever you need will be provided for you."

"How can I thank you, Father?" Kateri hung her head in humility. "I have so much to thank you for."

"No, child. It is God who is good. Here. I have prepared a letter for you to give to the priest at the Praying Castle."

Kateri took the envelope with trembling hands. She couldn't read, but she would take good care of it and deliver it as she was told.

Soon Karonhyate knocked on the door and entered with a smile for Kateri. His long gray hair half hid his face. He had draped a fur cape across his shoulders and it hid the lower part of his face.

"Little sister," he said, "we must leave quickly. Everything is ready and the canoe is waiting. We will depart while Iowerano is busy at the fort. Onas and Jacob are waiting at Big Rock. You will go first, but stay out of sight. I will follow."

Father de Lamberville blessed them with the Sign of the Cross. Kateri pulled her blanket over her head. She slipped out of the study and disappeared into the forest, hurrying to Big Rock where Onas and Jacob were waiting for her.

Walking close to the water's edge, but staying among the dense trees and bushes, Kateri made her way to the designated spot. Once she ducked behind a tree when two children came walking down a nearby path. As soon as they passed, she was on the move again. Karonhyate followed closely, his arms filled with supplies.

At Big Rock, Onas helped Kateri into an elm-bark canoe. As it moved from the shore and took Kateri away from Caughnawaga, she looked back with sadness. It was painful to leave the village she loved, but her heart sang with joy for the new life she was about to begin.

Kateri heard Onas's voice above the rush of the water. "We must make good time. We want to pass Fort Orange before Iowerano finishes his trading. When I tell you, Kateri, you must drop down onto the floor of the canoe and we'll cover you with this blanket. We cannot take any chances."

Onas kept a good lookout for Iowerano, but they didn't pass even one canoe along the way. When they neared Fort Orange, he gave the signal, "Now, Kateri, drop down!"

She did as she was told and Onas threw a blanket over her. In the darkness she imagined her stepfather on the shore outside the trading post. In her mind's eye, he looked angry. She knew that when Iowerano came home and found her gone, he would look just like that, his thin lips a straight line, his eyes bulging in rage and disbelief. He would certainly search for her, and if he found her, he would bring her back to Caughnawaga. He would probably find it hard to believe that anyone would dare defy him to help his stepdaughter escape. Despite the constant abuse she had suffered, her disappearance would be something of a mystery to him, to Karitha and Arosen, and perhaps even to the entire village.

Kateri shivered beneath the warm blanket. Though she had acted courageously, she was still afraid of her uncle. She didn't know what her punishment would be if Iowerano found her. But as she crouched to hide at the bottom of the canoe, she did know that she would gladly give her life for Rawanniio.

CHAPTER 15

SAFELY HOME

The canoe glided smoothly through the water. It passed through the rapids with the sureness of Mohawk skill, then sped along in the quiet river again. For two months, they patiently walked and paddled the two hundred miles. Kateri was weary but excited. When Onas said, "We are close to the village now," her heart began to pound so hard she could hear it beating in her ears.

When they arrived, Kateri stepped from the canoe and immediately found herself in the arms of Anastasia. The older woman's warm embrace enveloped Kateri in a circle of love and acceptance.

"Little Sunshine," said Anastasia. "You are home! You are safely home!" Her wet cheek met Kateri's rough face and they wept together.

At Sault-St. Louis a large wooden cross had been erected on the shore to mark the

"Little Sunshine, you are home!
You are safely home!"

Praying Castle. The Christian village had been moved twice. Now known as the St. Francis Xavier Mission du Sault, it was situated on the St. Lawrence River at the rapids across from Montreal.

Kateri was happy to see the familiar longhouses, exactly like the ones at Caughnawaga, but fewer. She was awestruck, however, at the church, which was similar to the one she had seen at Fort Orange. The golden steeple gleamed like a beacon in the sunlight.

The town was governed by four Indian leaders, and each household was managed by an older woman who made decisions for the family. Onas and Enita lived in the longhouse where Kateri would make her home. Anastasia was the head of that household. She made all the decisions for the household and met the spiritual needs of the family.

The house was much like Iowerano's longhouse. Kateri had her own little space, a bench, a sleeping shelf, and an animal skin partition for privacy.

"This is where you will stay," Anastasia said as she brought Kateri to a corner of the traditional dwelling. "These things are for you. You will have whatever you need.

There is very good trading at Ville Marie (Montreal)."

Kateri brought a gentle hand to a pile of soft skins. A basket of wampum and ribbons sat nearby. There were needles and stacks of woody bast fibers, leather, porcupine quills, and beads. "Everything I need for sewing," she said, her voice catching. "I am so grateful."

Anastasia smiled. "Your handiwork will support you, Kateri. That is, if you do not find a husband." She winked. "There are young men here, too."

Kateri looked down and shook her head. "I want only to be a Christian and worship God."

Anastasia frowned. "You are a strange one, Kateri. I will leave you now and prepare a meal. You must be hungry."

Kateri sighed. She felt peace within herself and with her surroundings. The fear that Iowerano might follow her here to the Praying Castle did not disturb her now. It was clear that Rawanniio was guiding her.

Kateri's bed was a layer of pine boughs covered with a soft deerskin. A warm fur was spread over it, and resting on the bed were new moccasins and squares of linen. Wampum hung against the wall above the bed and there were knives and tools for scraping and carving. Already Kateri was planning the things she would make to help support the family.

"*Segon, skennon gowa!* Welcome! Great peace be with you!" Kateri turned to face Enita.

Enita had grown plumper, and her face was radiant. "I am so happy you are here! I thought I would never see you again."

Enita hugged Kateri and then stood back and said. "How is our father and the family? I have prayed for them."

The mention of Iowerano, Karitha, and Arosen sent a shiver through her, but Kateri said, "They are in good health. The last corn harvest was better than usual, so there is enough to eat. The village has been safe."

"Thank God for that! From time to time we received bits of news from Father de Lamberville." Enita hugged Kateri again. "When we heard of your baptism, Kateri Tekakwitha, we were all so happy."

Kateri's face had suddenly lost its weariness. "Please take me to the chapel," she said. "I would like to offer my thanks to God there. I'll tell Anastasia that I will eat later."

CHAPTER 16

THE PRAYING CASTLE

The church was different from the chapel at Caughnawaga. Unlike the rough bark houses of the Christians, St. Francis Xavier was a large wooden building. On the very top was a gilded cross.

Kateri opened the door slowly and entered the chapel. The scent of candle wax and incense greeted her. She was alone, alone with the one true God.

"Oh, Rawanniio," she whispered, "I know you better now and I shall come to know you better still. I love you more than life itself. You are in my heart forever."

Shadows from the trees outside fell upon the windows and the church grew darker. Only the clang of the bells reminding the faithful to pray the Angelus roused Kateri, not the emptiness of hunger. Kateri stayed kneeling at the altar, thanking God for his goodness.

It was almost twilight when she heard a voice calling out, "Tekakwitha! Welcome." It was Father Fremin standing in the waning sunlight with two other blackrobes, Father Cholenec (SHO-le-nek) and Father Chauchetiere (Sho-shet-YAIR).

"Fathers," he said, turning toward the men, "this is Kateri Tekakwitha." He turned back to Kateri. "How you have grown, little one. You were a child when you served the priests in the house of Iowerano."

Kateri nodded and smiled. "This is from Father de Lamberville," she said, removing the letter from a pocket on her tunic.

Father Fremin read the letter and passed it to the two other priests. They exchanged glances as Father Fremin folded it and tucked it under his arm. "As soon as you are settled, Kateri, Father Cholenec will give you instructions for First Communion. You may receive the Sacrament on Christmas."

Kateri Tekakawitha took a little breath and held it. The joy in her heart spread across her face in a smile. She crossed her arms against her chest and bowed her head. "God is so good to me. How could I ever ask him for anything more?"

"Go with God, Kateri," Father Fremin said, and Tekakwitha hurried home.

Anastasia's hot meal of venison, beans, corn, and bear grease brought Kateri's strength rushing back. She was flushed with happiness and gratitude. She had not heard an angry voice, nor had she been greeted with any disapproving looks. Everyone at the Praying Castle welcomed her.

Kateri's days were filled with household duties, instructions in the faith, and worship. Anastasia and Kateri were inseparable. When the villagers saw one, the other was nearby. The older woman's duty was to instruct her household in spiritual matters and Kateri was most eager to learn.

A few days before Christmas the first heavy snow of the season fell upon the Praying Castle. The longhouses, the church, the tall wooden cross on the shore, the trees, and the footpaths, all were covered with a white blanket. Anastasia had laid aside a white woolen veil for Kateri Tekakwitha to wear at her First Communion.

The women decorated the church with pine boughs and red berries, rich beaver pelts and furs. The rakeni had taught carols to the children in their own language. As Kateri approached the altar they sang, their voices as sweet as those of angels. It was as if the cherubim had descended from heaven to sing at Kateri Tekakwitha's First Holy Communion.

The aura of her first Confession remained with her. As she knelt to receive the Body and Blood of Christ, tears streamed down her cheeks. She bowed her head and knelt transfixed, for she believed that God dwelled within her. Never had she known such perfect happiness.

When Mass ended, the people quietly left the church—all but Kateri. She wanted to hold onto this special moment for as long as possible. Winter would be long, and she would not receive Holy Communion again until Easter. That was the custom.

The cold winds spawned in the north blew swiftly off the river, and during the night everything froze. The ice on the St. Lawrence was thick enough to walk on, and it was time for the winter hunt to begin.

CHAPTER 17

THE WINTER HUNT

Kateri longed to stay at home where Mass would be celebrated daily, but only elderly and ill persons would be allowed to stay. The blackrobes would care for those who remained. Though Kateri wished with all her heart to be close to the chapel and the tabernacle within, she was needed on the trail. She accompanied Onas, Enita, and their children willingly.

The hunting party left the village on a dreary morning when the sky was leaden gray and snow was falling, trudging into the depths of the snowy forest. Kateri looked back at the church and raised her eyes to the golden cross. She turned back again and again until the cross was out of sight. Pulling her thin blanket tighter, Kateri bowed her head and followed the rest.

In the afternoon the group stopped to set up camp in a clearing. All hands were needed, and Kateri helped Enita and the women gather pine boughs for temporary shelters.

Onas built a framework and piled the pine brush around it. Skins were spread over all, and though the dwelling was not as snug as the longhouse, it made a cozy home. The women spent much of their time outdoors, preparing meat and tanning hides. While the men hunted, the women would enjoy some leisure, telling stories about past events and catching up on the latest news. When the men returned, they were too exhausted to do anything but sleep. That is when the women's work began.

Kateri missed the church of St. Francis Xavier at the Praying Castle. Sometimes, when she knew her absence wouldn't be noticed, she slipped away to the woods and prayed as she used to do. She often knelt in the snow until her legs were so numb she could hardly walk. Kateri lashed two pieces of wood together to make a cross. Now she understood what the cross meant, and she wept when she thought of Christ's suffering.

When Kateri returned to camp, a blustering wind whipped the frame house, whistling through the cracks and down the smoke hole. The women huddled inside, praying the men would come home safely.

"The men will be late," Enita said. "The wind will slow them down."

"They will be too tired to eat," a woman named Seceweda said, "but we'll leave cornmeal and beans in the pot for them anyway."

It grew dark earlier than usual and the women bedded down for the night. They drew what little warmth they could from the cookfire. Finally the men returned.

The women worked for more than four days, but finally the meat had been prepared and the skins hung between trees or over branches. Onas announced that soon they would return to the village. Kateri smiled. More than anything she wanted to go back to St. Francis Xavier and to the tall cross on the shore.

The day before the hunting party began the trek back to the Praying Castle, the women sat in the sunshine repairing moccasins, shirts, and tunics. The weather was cold, but warmer than it had been, and the sun felt good on Kateri's shoulders. As usual, the women chattered—and gossiped. Kateri asked, "Do any of you know the new hymn Father Fremin taught us? Sing it with me."

The small group of noisy women set aside their tales and found themselves singing with Kateri, praising God the Father. Her voice could be heard a little above all the others.

That hymn ended and Kateri was about to start another when Seceweda's husband Louis came out to the group of women. He smiled at Kateri. "Would you be so kind as to sew a part of the canoe I am making? It's a difficult task and you are best when it comes to the needle."

Kateri, always happy and willing to help, and without thinking, said, "I'll sew whatever you wish."

Seceweda sucked in her breath and her nostrils flared. Kateri didn't realize that this jealous woman saw something evil in her answer.

Returning to the Mission du Sault, Kateri couldn't have been happier. Some members of the party returned in canoes filled with dried meats, furs, and skins. Kateri joined those who trudged back on tired feet, but when she caught sight of the golden cross on the steeple she began to run. Hurrying to the church she knelt at the altar and prayed. "Thank you, Rawanniio, for a good hunt and for bringing us back safely. I have missed your presence in the tabernacle, yet I know you were with me the whole time away."

Kateri remained in the cold, unheated church, her hands folded and her head bowed. She stayed until the shadows fell and the light no longer came through the windows. Only then did she get up and return home. But as she left, she saw Seceweda knocking at the door of Father Fremin's study. The door opened and Kateri heard Father Fremin say, "Welcome home from the hunt, Seceweda. You look upset. Is something wrong?"

"I must speak to you, Father," Seceweda answered. "Something happened on the hunt."

"Come in, child, come in," said Father Fremin. "Tell me what is troubling you."

The door closed and Kateri stood on the steps of the chapel feeling very alone and very sad.

CHAPTER 18

ACCUSATIONS AND DENIAL

Kateri stared at the calendar on the wall above Father Fremin's head. It pictured Mary, the Mother of God. She wore a blue head covering, and Kateri was surprised that it looked much like her own.

"Kateri, I have a few questions I must ask you. I beg you to please answer them truthfully."

Kateri noted the serious tone of his voice. "Yes, Father, of course."

"During your stay at the winter camp, did you go in the forest alone each day? And did you do so secretly, hoping no one would notice you?"

Kateri answered with a simple, "Yes."

Father Fremin continued, "Did you meet someone in the forest and talk to him?"

Kateri's cheeks reddened at Father's words, but she remained calm.

"Yes, Father, I spoke to someone, but it was not a man. I went each day to pray to Jesus, to spend time with him each day. I wish to keep this a secret, so please do not tell the other women. It doesn't matter if they suspect me of evil. My soul must answer to God alone."

Father Fremin smiled. "Dry your eyes, little one. In the letter you delivered, Father de Lamberville wrote that your soul is very close to the Lord. He said that we would soon realize what a jewel he sent to us. We all know that, Kateri. Go with God."

Father Fremin made the Sign of the Cross in blessing and Kateri quietly left his study. But her heart was broken. To be falsely accused here, at the Praying Castle, and by another Christian, was unthinkable. Kateri was not looking for a husband—not her own or anyone else's.

As the days went by, Anastasia stayed close to Kateri Tekakwitha. It had been her duty to tutor the girl in the faith and she was determined to do it well.

"Kateri," she said one summer day as the two of them gathered wild berries, "we should do more penance for our sins."

"Yes, Anastasia," Kateri answered. "Jesus died to forgive sins. I know that I am a poor and unworthy sinner. At least I can show him I'm grateful by offering little sacrifices out of love."

Kateri looked into the bucket of luscious berries. They were red and ripe and smelled sweetly. It would have been so wonderful to pop a handful into her mouth, especially since she was thirsty and hungry. Instead she chose to deny herself, stifle the desire, and offer a silent prayer as she searched for more berries.

The next morning before sunrise, Kateri was walking along a path to the woods not often used by the villagers. The day was just dawning when she found the spot she had planned to make her own special place of prayer. Taking out her knife, Kateri began to carve a cross on the trunk of a great tree. Suddenly the weather turned. The fury of the wind whipped her hair against her face and blew the blanket from her head and shoulders. Freezing rain pelted her body. With stiff fingers, she continued to carve the cross. When she was finished she stood back, knelt on the cold ground, and began to pray. *I can't give you all that you deserve, Jesus. But I can give you this time, and all the love in my heart.*

The church on Easter Sunday was decorated with wildflowers. Mass was offered early in the morning and the entire village took part. The wooden church was crowded with Christians, so many that there was not enough room for all of them. Construction of a new church—made of stone—had begun close by. Almost finished, the building was the pride of the village.

On this Sunday, Kateri, for the second time, was allowed to receive the Holy Eucharist. She came away from the altar rail with her face in her hands and her shoulders shaking. She wept for joy to receive the one true God, Rawanniio, to whom Kateri had dedicated her life.

Anastasia turned toward Kateri and saw that she was sobbing. There was something about this girl, whom she loved as a daughter, that was like no one else. Anastasia thought about the day Kateri Tekakwitha was born, and all the days and years that followed. It seemed to her that a mysterious holiness set Kateri apart. This small girl possessed a heroic and courageous spirit, one that Anastasia didn't fully understand.

The cloud of incense gradually disappeared, but its fragrance hung in the air and mingled with the scent of candle wax. One by one the people shuffled out of the dark church. Anastasia gently tapped Kateri on the shoulder. "Come, Kateri, it is time to go home and prepare our feast for the rakeni."

Kateri roused herself, looked up, and smiled at Anastasia. "In my remaining days I must do whatever is most pleasing to God."

Anastasia gazed at Kateri with wonder. Her words were unsettling.

CHAPTER 19

INSEPARABLE FRIENDS

As time passed it became clear that the focus of Kateri's entire life was pleasing God. In every task, no matter how simple, she found a way to love him. The new stone church was finished except for a few details, and Kateri was drawn to it. Setting her sewing aside, she left the longhouse, walked to the church, and went inside. The interior was cool and dim. It smelled of fresh lumber and paint. She stood in the aisle, squinting at the new pews, the communion rail, and the hand-carved altar. Beautiful Stations of the Cross, which helped her recall the passion of Christ, were all in place. The only sound was the tap-tapping of a workman's hammer completing some final task.

Kateri didn't need to turn around to sense that someone was standing in the aisle behind her. The presence of whoever it was felt comforting, as if God had sent someone to keep her company.

"This is such a beautiful church," a woman's voice said in the language of the

Oneida people. Kateri understood the words, and nodded in agreement. Then speaking aloud her inner thoughts, she said, "This chapel *is* beautiful, but God truly wishes to make his home in our hearts."

The woman wondered if Kateri knew her story . . . But how could she? They had never met before.

"Can we sit down over there on the big stones? There is something I wish to tell you," asked the woman.

The pain of a bitter memory crossed the woman's face as she began to tell her story.

"I am Marie Therese. I was baptized a Catholic as a young girl, but after my marriage to a non-Christian man, I fell away from my faith. My husband's relatives did not approve of Catholics, and they encouraged me to drink whiskey and join in the festivals of their gods. I did not have the courage to go against them. May God forgive me for all the sins I've committed."

Tears of sorrow filled Marie Therese's eyes as she recalled her foolishness. Taking a deep breath, she continued.

"When my sister moved to the La Prairie settlement, I convinced my husband that we should also move there. Being near other Christians made it easier for me to live my faith, but then the urge for whiskey again led me to sin. By the time of the winter hunt, I had been away from the sacraments for many months.

"We started out in the early autumn, but soon our food supply ran low. Then heavy snowfalls made hunting impossible. Hunger plagued us. We lived only on the bark of trees and roots and struggled on, not knowing how we would be able to continue.

"My husband became very sick and died. His last words were full of regret that he had not let the blackrobes baptize him. I felt more alone then than ever before. Yet more frightening than my loneliness or sorrow was the thought that I too might die without having a chance to confess my sins. I prayed and begged Rawanniio to spare me so I could do penance for my past life of sin."

Kateri listened intently as Marie Therese continued.

"At last, the hunters caught a wolf, and the meat sustained those of us who were left until we reached the Ottawa River. During the last days of the trip we were again without food, but it didn't matter. I knew we would soon be in La Prairie. There I found the blackrobes. They gave us food, but also fed my starved soul."

Marie Therese's head had been down while she related her story. Now slowly she raised it so their eyes could meet. Kateri's face was full of understanding compassion, without a trace of scorn or shock. Her shy smile gave Marie Therese a new surge of courage and resolution.

"Marie Therese," whispered Kateri, "God has been very good to you as he has to me. Perhaps we can live a life of prayer and penance together to express our gratitude to him."

Kateri and Marie Therese soon became inseparable friends. Together they worked in the fields, prayed, and shared the desire to spend their lives entirely for God.

One June morning, Marie Therese came to share some exciting news.

"Kateri, two canoes will leave today for Ville Marie (VEEya ma-REE) where our deerskin blankets, wampum belts, and moccasins can be sold at the market. But while the others are busy taking care of the

*"Perhaps we can live a life of prayer
and penance together . . ."*

trading, you and I can visit the holy French women who care for sick people at the Hotel-Dieu (o-TEL deeUH)."

Kateri quickly agreed to Marie Therese's plan. They had often heard people talk about the holy women who served at the hospital. Father Cholenec called them "sisters," but neither Kateri nor Marie Therese knew much about them.

The religious sisters at the Hotel-Dieu greeted the two young women and gave them a tour of the hospital. Both French and native Indian patients were given the same loving care. As they passed from one room to another, Marie Therese asked their guide many questions. She was told that the Sisters of the Hotel-Dieu, like the Sisters of Notre Dame who taught at a school in Montreal, had dedicated their lives entirely to God. They dressed alike, lived together, had certain hours dedicated to prayer, and made a vow of virginity.

"A vow of virginity . . ." Kateri's shy voice repeated the sister's last words. She hoped to fully understand what such words meant.

"Yes, my dear," Sister further explained. "We do not marry so that we can give our love and our lives to God alone. Through the grace of this total consecration to God we are able to love him and our neighbor completely."

Tears of joy welled up in Kateri's eyes. She had never heard anyone express the desires that she had kept carefully locked in her heart. No one had understood her reason for not marrying; not even she had understood it fully. But now she could dedicate herself to Jesus anew with a solemn promise, a vow that would be a gift of herself to God as an eternal Spouse.

CHAPTER 20

NOT GOD'S WILL

For weeks after their return from Ville Marie, Kateri and Marie Therese spoke of nothing else but their visit to the sisters. They were both ablaze with new ideas and plans.

"Kateri," Marie Therese exclaimed one day, "why can't we start our own convent somewhere near the village? We could live apart from the others, and pray and work as do the sisters in Ville Marie. By selling our belts and moccasins, we would have the means to help others, especially those who are poor or sick."

"That's a wonderful idea, Marie Therese, but maybe we should ask someone else to join us, someone who knows more about how to be a sister."

Marie Therese thought for a moment and then said, "I know who—Marie Skarichions (ska-LEE-shoos). She's older and used to live at the mission called Our Lady of Loretto in Quebec."

The three women met to discuss their plans. As Marie Therese had thought, Marie Skarichions's acquaintance with the nuns in Quebec had given her a practical knowledge of convent life.

"Now we must decide where our convent should be," concluded Marie Therese enthusiastically.

Looking across the river, her eyes fell on the Island of Herons. "Oh, that would be the perfect place," Marie Therese exclaimed, answering her own inquiry.

As Kateri listened to every word of their conversation, an important thought suddenly came to her.

"There is one more thing we should do before we go ahead with our plans."

"What's that, Kateri?" the other two asked.

"We must be sure that our idea is God's will and not just ours. We must tell Father Fremin what we have discussed and accept whatever advice he gives us."

They agreed and sent Kateri to Father as their representative.

Father Fremin broke into a wide smile as Kateri revealed their plan. The fervor with which she spoke touched his heart, but the impracticability of such an idea turned his smile into a subdued chuckle.

Kateri was somewhat surprised by the priest's reaction. He met her questioning gaze with words spoken gently from true fatherly love.

"My dear Kateri, I'm sure our Lord is pleased with the holy desires of your soul. But I don't believe the plan you have just described is what he wants for you. Religious communities are not founded overnight, nor by those who are still young in the faith. Be content to live with your families. Give them good example and pray for them. This is what Rawanniio wants of you."

Kateri returned to the others with her disappointing news. They accepted it as wisdom and a matter of obedience, and they let go of their idea of a "convent" on Heron Island.

Kateri kept herself neatly dressed but avoided wearing beaded necklaces and wampum ornaments. She wore her hair parted in the middle with a braid down the back. Ever since receiving Holy Communion, she had worn a simple blue blanket over her dress and leggings.

While Kateri and her two companions had been speaking about starting a religious community, others had been talking about an entirely different subject.

Kateri's friends, who knew nothing of her desire to belong only to Jesus, still hoped that she would find a good husband. They were certain that Kateri did not realize what hardships and difficulties would be hers if she did not marry soon.

Anastasia and Enita decided to take action. "Of course you are right, Enita. But have you noticed that Kateri cares little about her appearance?" Anastasia observed. "She does not oil her hair. Her clothes are old and unattractive. We must speak to her."

When Kateri entered the longhouse, Anastasia and Enita sat her down on one of the low benches. Although they had Kateri's best interests at heart, they began to pressure her by making all the arguments they could think of in favor of marriage.

"I know of the ordeal you suffered when your aunt and uncle tried to trick you into a marriage with a Mohawk brave, but the young men of our village are all fine Christians. I know of more than one who would be pleased to have you for a wife."

Kateri shook her head, but since she owed much to Anastasia and Enita she listened politely. They deserved her love and respect.

"Thank you for your concern for my welfare. But don't worry, my needs are small. I will pray about what you've said."

Anastasia sighed with relief. "There is hope, Enita. At least Kateri didn't refuse the proposition altogether. But I must say something more."

Anastasia's voice was full of concern. "Kateri, do you realize how your strange behavior causes people to talk? It isn't normal for a Mohawk girl to remain unmarried. You should obey your elders in this."

Kateri could no longer control the flow of tears that had been pushing themselves forward with each of Anastasia's words. Yet there was still only one answer she could give.

"I do *not* wish to marry . . . I will *not* marry. Please do not speak to me again about this, Anastasia. It is God who knows what is best for me."

Kateri left the women and ran to see Father Cholenec. He would understand and help her.

"Father Cholenec, may I speak with you? There is something important I must tell you."

"I always have time for my spiritual children. Come in, Kateri. How can I help you?"

"Father, some of the women will not stop talking to me about marriage. They insist that I must find a husband. I know they mean well . . . but Father, how can I marry a man when my heart belongs to Jesus alone? I want to give my whole life to him as the sisters in Ville Marie do. Father, may I make a vow of virginity?"

Father Cholenec was astonished at Kateri's words. What she was asking had not been requested by any Mohawk before her. For years he had labored among the people of different tribes, content to see them embrace the Catholic faith. But here before him was a young woman who had gone far beyond his simple instruction—a woman who aspired to a life of total consecration to God.

"My dear Kateri, how pleased our Lord must be with the generous gift you so greatly desire to offer him. Be in peace, it will not be taken from you."

Kateri's face became radiant with joy. Father Cholenec set March 25, the Feast of the Annunciation, as the day on which she would make her vow. It was several months away, so she would have time to prepare for this solemn day with prayer and penance. She thanked the missionary priest and ran to share the news with her closest friend, Marie Therese.

CHAPTER 21

A VOW OF LOVE

Kateri's prepared for her spiritual "wedding day" with additional penances, prayers, and acts of charity. She was extravagant with the sacrifices she offered, fasting often and even mixing her food with ashes to deaden the taste. Constantly looking for ways to give God even more, she said her rosary as she walked barefoot in the snow, attended two Masses each morning, and returned to chapel in the afternoon, praying and meditating for hours.

Nor were Kateri's acts of charity any less. She gathered a group of twelve other young women for weekly meetings and instructed them about the practice of virtues. Kateri encouraged the women to talk with each other in a helpful way about their faults.

They also took care of others in the village who were sick or poor by gathering bundles of firewood, working on wampum belts, and grinding corn. Kateri cared for the needs of others with such tenderness and generosity that the head of the Jesuit missionaries called her an "angel of charity."

Finally, on March 25, 1679, the Mohawk and Algonquin bride was ready to meet her heavenly Bridegroom.

Father Cholenec celebrated the 8:00 AM Mass. Kneeling serenely in one of the front pews was Kateri. After receiving Jesus in Holy Communion, she spent a few moments in thanksgiving and then pronounced her vow of virginity.

"My dear Jesus, freely and willingly do I solemnly renounce the happiness of married life in order to have you alone as my Spouse.

"Holy Mother of God, present me to your divine Son. Be my Mother. I wish to always be your obedient and faithful daughter. Help me, dear Mother, help me."

It was one of the happiest and most beautiful days of Kateri's life.

Marie Therese and Kateri found a deserted cabin not far from the village. A French fur trapper had abandoned it years before, and the building had been ravaged by the elements. Though the place had a hearth,

Kateri and Marie Therese chose to do penance by praying without heat, even in the coldest weather. They knelt on the hard earthen floor while snow drifted in from the windows and doorway. Here they worshipped and offered sacrifice.

Kateri even went so far as to secretly put prickly branches from a brier bush under her mat so that she could share more fully in the suffering of Jesus. She offered this penance for the conversion of her people in the Mohawk valley.

"Rawanniio, use my pain to bring the light of truth to my people. I know that sins offend you, but I ask for your mercy. Oh, my crucified Jesus, how I desire to suffer with you for the sake of their souls!"

These extreme acts of penance in addition to Kateri's already weak health left her in a state of total exhaustion. Marie Therese, who had joined Kateri in so many other practices of penance, became frightened by Kateri's condition.

"Kateri," Marie Therese said with great concern, "I cannot help but see how weak you are. You are hardly able to walk. What are you doing to yourself? I know it must be some new penance. Tell me, Kateri. We've never kept secrets from each other."

Kateri pulled back the covers of her mat and revealed the thorn branches that were responsible for her sleepless nights.

"But Kateri," protested Marie Therese, "Rawanniio does not want you to harm yourself. You must ask your confessor's permission and advice."

Marie Therese's words startled her. The thought that she might be doing something wrong had never entered her mind. She immediately went to Father Cholenec. While her motives filled the priest with admiration, he knew it was his duty to correct her misunderstanding.

"Kateri," he said seriously, "you are to go back to your cabin and throw those branches into the fire. This is not what God wants. Your heart is enough for him."

"Yes, Father, I will do as you say."

As he watched her hobble away, Father Cholenec praised God for Kateri's deep spirit of obedience. The will of God was supreme in her life; the secret of the saints had become her own.

Kateri was usually in her cabin or in church. Whenever she was needed she was always ready to help. She made five visits each day to the chapel and nothing kept her from that practice, even on days when she was not well. When she could, Kateri cared for others. But the smallpox she had suffered early in life and the harsh penances she had chosen for herself had taken their toll.

As the year wore on, Kateri's health continued to fail. Father Cholenec, aware that Kateri was losing strength, brought a group of children to visit her.

"You need rest from constant prayer," he said. "I will give the children their lesson here where you can listen without tiring yourself."

He told the stories of Scripture as if he were painting pictures. Father Cholenec explained the lessons carefully, and the children, as well as Kateri, grew in their understanding. When the session was over, the children sang hymns and Mohawk songs Kateri remembered from childhood. She smiled as she lay back against the soft skins. "Please, Father, bring the children back tomorrow."

"I will, Kateri," Father Cholenec assured her. "They enjoyed their visit as much as you did."

All through Lent the children received their lessons at Kateri's bedside. She grew noticeably weaker each day, and her voice became a mere whisper. Anastasia hovered in the shadows, watchful and silent. Marie Therese had to join the other women in the fields, but whenever she could, she came to Kateri's bedside. The two friends prayed together, only now Marie Therese prayed more fervently. Frightened by the thought of losing her friend, she offered more penances to God and asked him to make Kateri strong again.

CHAPTER 22

FACE TO FACE

Since the beginning of Lent, Kateri had been too weak to go to the chapel. On Tuesday of Holy Week, Father Fremin paid Kateri a visit.

In a voice that was barely a whisper she asked, "Father, is it true what they say? Am I going to die?" She smiled. "I will see Rawanniio's face then, won't I?"

Father Cholenec tried to speak, but bit his lip and closed his eyes for a moment.

"I think you will see Rawanniio soon, Kateri."

Her face became radiant at the reply. "I will be happy to leave," she said, "but first I want to receive Holy Communion again."

The priest brought both hands together in a gesture of prayer and lifted them to his lips. He seemed to be pondering something.

"It has always been the custom for the sick and the dying to be brought to the church to receive the Blessed Sacrament, but you are too weak. I will talk to the fathers.

We must make an exception for you. We will bring Jesus to you."

An expression of pure happiness spread across Kateri's face. "Then I will die happily," she whispered.

The sun lit the path to Kateri's longhouse on this early spring day. Father Cholenec, followed by village men, women, and children, brought the Blessed Sacrament to Kateri. The people waited outside the door. Some knelt, some prayed, some stood silently. All grieved. All wanted to be with her to the end.

Kateri received the Holy Eucharist, her eyes closed, a smile on her lips. Those who had waited outside now joined in prayer. One by one they came and went, anxious to see Kateri one last time.

Kateri's face was sweet and peaceful. She lay back upon the bed, silent and still. Father Cholenec prepared to administer the last rites. But Kateri opened her eyes and whispered, "It is not yet time, Father, not yet time."

Marie Therese stayed with Kateri throughout the evening. Her heart was breaking with grief. Suddenly Kateri opened her eyes and smiled. "I know very well, my sister, what I am saying. I know where you came from, and I know what you were doing there. Take courage! You may be sure that God is pleased with you, and I will help you more when I am with him."

Marie Therese was startled by the words. "Kateri, you know all about me, even things I never told you! I love you and I want to be with you to the end. But I must work tomorrow and I am afraid you will die while I am away."

"Go to the field, Marie Therese; don't worry. You will be back in time."

But Kateri's soul was slipping away, like autumn leaves falling softly to earth. One of the blackrobes gave her the last rites of the Church, and Enita sent for Marie Therese. The words that fell from Kateri's lips were hardly audible. Marie Therese leaned closer.

"I am going to die," said Kateri. "I will love you in heaven . . ."

The Indians who had gathered inside and outside her cabin now began to file past her one by one. "Don't forget us, little sister. Tell Rawanniio of our needs. He will listen to you."

Kateri, who had always been shy and reserved, was still able to find the right words for each person. "I will pray for you . . . Pray for my poor soul, too . . . Be strong in our faith . . . Love Jesus. . . . Love Mary. . . ."

Kateri reached for her crucifix and brought it to her lips. Her expression was one of pure joy. "Jesus, Mary—I love you," she whispered and then closed her eyes.

Kateri Tekakwitha died on Wednesday, April 17, 1680. She was twenty-four years old.

Father Cholenec and Father Chauchetiere had been reciting prayers for the dying in Kateri's last moments. Most people present seemed unable to move away. Father Chauchetiere watched Kateri's face with astonishment. In moments her face became instantly beautiful. The scars from the small-pox she had borne all her life suddenly disappeared, and her skin became radiant. Kateri's people gasped. This beautiful flower of faith belonged to them.

Anastasia, recalling the horrible small pox epidemic that had taken place so many years ago, gazed at Kateri's face and exclaimed, "Little Sunshine!"

Before the people left the cabin, they filed passed Kateri's body. Many reached out to touch her hand, or gently stroke her cheek. They felt as if by doing so they might bring their own souls closer to God.

When everyone had left, Marie Therese, Enita, and Anastasia prepared Kateri for burial. They combed, oiled, and braided her hair. They washed her body and put on clean and beautiful garments. They put new moccasins on her feet and laid her upon a fresh mat. Again the visitors came.

Two Frenchmen arrived in the village to pay their respects. They had remembered Kateri from other visits to the Sault. To them she was the Indian girl who lived like a nun. But seeing her now in such a beautiful state was beyond their comprehension. One of them said, "This Christian heroine must be buried in the manner of our own nuns. We'll build a coffin for this blessed flower of the forest, this Lily of the Mohawks!"

On Thursday afternoon of Holy Week, Kateri Tekakwitha was tenderly placed in a coffin and lowered into her grave. The site was one she had once chosen for herself. It was the spot beneath the tall cross near the river. This cross had inspired and comforted her when she first arrived at the Praying Castle. At the foot of this cross she had come so often to pray.

EPILOGUE

Pope John Paul II beatified Kateri Tekakwitha in 1980, the three-hundreth anniversary year of her death. She was the first North American Indian to be declared Blessed. Saint Kateri was canonized by Pope Benedict XVI on October 21, 2012, during the Year of Faith. Her willingness to suffer rejection and cruelty because of her faith, and her courage in seeking Baptism at great personal cost, has inspired many people. Saint Kateri is the patroness of ecology and the environment, and of people bullied because of their faith. Her feast day is July 14.

The National Shrine of Saint Kateri Tekakwitha in the United States is in Fonda, New York. Another shrine honoring Saint Kateri is located in Auriesville, New York, at the National Shrine of Our Lady of the Martyrs. This holy place is dedicated to the memory of those who gave their lives to bring the Gospel of Jesus Christ to the peoples of North America. Saint Kateri's tomb remains at St. Francis Xavier Church in Kahnawake, Quebec, Canada.

PRAYER

May the Holy Spirit bless me as I pray.

Saint Kateri Tekakwitha, you waited many years to be baptized and to receive Jesus in the Holy Eucharist, but never lost hope. May I have the patience to wait for what is best for me, and overcome all the obstacles that keep me from God.

As a young person you showed great courage, standing up for your faith among people who did not share it. May I find strength in difficult times and deeply trust in God who hears and answers me.

Saint Kateri, you learned God's will for your life, and followed his plan with all your heart.

May the Holy Spirit give me a heart like yours, filled with love for Jesus and ready to serve others.

Pray for me, Saint Kateri, that as long as I live I may be like you, and walk the path of goodness that leads me to heaven even when I cannot see the way.

This I ask through Christ, our Lord. Amen.

GLOSSARY

You may have noticed that Mohawk words are pronounced quite differently from what you might expect.

1. **Ayonwatha**—a great Iroquois chief whom the Mohawks claimed as their own. He is more commonly known as Hiawatha.

2. **Caughnawaga**—the village near present day Fonda, New York, where Kateri lived with her uncle's family after her own family had died.

3. **Fort Orange**—early name for the city of Albany, New York.

4. **Gan-a-shote**—a Mohawk word meaning, the cornstalk is standing.

5. **Ho-de-no-sau-nee**—an Onondaga word which means "they build longhouses," used to refer to the Iroquois.

6. **La Prairie**—a town in Canada in which early converts to Catholic Christianity settled.

7. **Iroquois**—Indians of the Five Great Nations: the Onondagas, Oneidas, Senecas, Cayugas, and Mohawks.

8. **Kahnawake**—village in Quebec, Canada, where the Mission of St. Francis Xavier was located.

9. **The League**—the Five Great Nations united to govern the tribes; this system of government influenced the founders of the United States.

10. **Longhouse**—a long communal dwelling made of bark and wood used by several North American tribes, especially those in the northeast.

11. **Okis**—evil spirits.

12. **Orenda**—a set of rules for the Iroquois to live by.

13. **Ossernenon**—the Mohawk town where Saint Kateri was born, now Auriesville, New York.

14. **Praying Castle**—the name Indian Catholics called the Church of St. Francis Xavier at Mission du Sault-Saint Louis.

15. **Rakeni**—blackrobes or blackgowns; the French priests of the Jesuit order.

16. **Rawanniio**—Indian word for the one true God; the God the Jesuit fathers brought to the native peoples of North America.

17. **Sault**—French word for rapids or falls.

18. **Shaman**—a tribal medicine man or spiritual healer.

19. **Smallpox**—an infectious disease that causes permanent scarring, blindness, and possibly death.

20. **Ville Marie**—present-day Montreal, Canada, an early French settlement.

21. **Vow of virginity**—a solemn promise not to marry for the sake of giving one's life only to God.

22. **Wampum**—strings of small white or purple shells. With the coming of Europeans, the beads were often made of glass. They represented peace, storytelling, and tribal history. They were also used as decorations or money.

BOOKS & MEDIA

The Daughters of St. Paul operate book and media centers at the following addresses. Visit, call, or write the one nearest you today, or find us at www.paulinestore.org.

CALIFORNIA
3908 Sepulveda Blvd, Culver City, CA 90230 — 310-397-8676
3250 Middlefield Road, Menlo Park, CA 94025 — 650-562-7060

FLORIDA
145 S.W. 107th Avenue, Miami, FL 33174 — 305-559-6715

HAWAII
1143 Bishop Street, Honolulu, HI 96813 — 808-521-2731

ILLINOIS
172 North Michigan Avenue, Chicago, IL 60601 — 312-346-4228

LOUISIANA
4403 Veterans Memorial Blvd, Metairie, LA 70006 — 504-887-7631

MASSACHUSETTS
885 Providence Hwy, Dedham, MA 02026 — 781-326-5385

MISSOURI
9804 Watson Road, St. Louis, MO 63126 — 314-965-3512

NEW YORK
115 E. 29th Street, New York City, NY 10016 — 212-754-1110

SOUTH CAROLINA
243 King Street, Charleston, SC 29401 — 843-577-0175

VIRGINIA
1025 King Street, Alexandria, VA 22314 — 703-549-3806

CANADA
3022 Dufferin Street, Toronto, ON M6B 3T5 — 416-781-9131